Butterflies

Whatever your passion is in life…

Feel Butterflies!

by

DiAndra Liccardo

ISBN-978-1-960853-12-7

Liberation's Publishing LLC
West Point - Mississippi

These poems came from a place of inspiration, of seeing love, wanting love, being in love, and most of all believing in love. I hope that as you read them that they create butterflies in your stomach and love in your heart.

−DiAndra

Table of Content

Dedication

I dedicate this book to the ones that touch my heart the most. The ones who are always by my side. I love you and thank you for believing in me.

Hard to Contain

Hard to contain

They flutter when they hear your name

The scent of you … excites them

With your touch … they'll never fly away

You give me butterflies that are here to stay.

More Time

I wish we had more time

Time to feel

Time to kiss

Time to really see if its

Each other that we miss

I wish we had more time

Time to hold

Time to squeeze

Time to realize

Why you're always in my dreams

I wish we had more time

Time to explore

Time to caress

Time to run to each other

When life is such a mess

I wish we had more time

Because maybe we would see

That true love does have a meaning

It begins with you and me.

Your Lips

Your lips

Pressed against mine

I want to feel that

All the time

The feel of your hands

The smell of your scent

Everything about you

I simply can't resist.

Fated

Can it be fate

Or maybe

Just wrong timing

It's hard to say

When I can't stop smiling

Not knowing you

But feeling like I do

My love life was darkened blue

But in vivid color when

I imagine you

Time changes quickly

And I can only seem to think

Why now

Why not sooner

Did our lips have to meet

Beyond control

Two souls met

My mind is curious

Of what will happen next.

Passion

Make love to me under the stars

Kiss me in the rain

Slow dance with me in the moonlight

Take my breath away

Hold me in your arms

You make me feel safe

Together we have passion

A passion we can't escape.

Waiting

For you I anxiously wait

To hear your voice

To kiss your lips

To feel your hands upon my skin

I love how you make me feel

You give me a feeling

That feels so unreal

A feeling I love

A feeling hard to resist.

Once you kiss me
There's no turning back
I'm addicted to you in every way
I lose all my control.

Wherever you are
The butterflies will follow
They lead me to you every time.

Love Quotes

Explore

Kiss me hard

Make love to me slow

Hold me tight

Don't let go

Tell me your thoughts

I want to know your dreams

The night is ours

Just you and me

Relax my mind

Free my soul

Have your way with me

Take control

My feelings are real

Hard to conceal

Burning with passion

Close your eyes and imagine.

More butterflies please.

Addicted

It's like my lips were made for yours

Because I long for your kiss everyday

The butterflies I feel when

I think of you

I've tried

But they won't go away

I think you're my weakness

Because you're all that I crave.

Speak into my mouth with kisses

You'll feed the butterflies.

Take Me Away

My greatest escape from reality

Is being in your arms

Happily in your presence

Is where my heart belongs

My greatest escape from reality

Is laying skin to skin

Staying up all night

Until the stars shine bright

As we hold each other's hand

My greatest escape from reality

Is you showering me with your love

As the water flows upon us

Hands on me like a fitted glove

My greatest escape from reality

Is looking into your eyes

My head against your chest

You got me at my best

My greatest escape from reality

Is kissing you a thousand times

As our bodies intertwine

In these moments

You are mine

My greatest escape from reality

Is simply being around you.

The Apex

Ignited by your flame

You're the one to blame

A passion so desirable

Hooked

Unstoppable

I get aroused by just the thought of you

Shivering

Quivering

Overdosed on you.

Desire

Anticipation

Of wanting you so bad

Thoughts of your kisses

Got me lost in a trance

No one knows

That my heart has thrills

Even the sound of your voice

Gives my body chills

I want to feel this way forever

You give my body pleasure.

Under the night sky

Beneath a thousand stars

I'll wait for you

To be with me

Wherever you are.

Wishing

If a genie

Could grant me a wish

My wish would be with you

I love everything about you

My only wish is you.

I Wish You Love

I hope you find that girl

Who is perfect

Just for you

The one that looks forward

To your text and calls

The way that I do

I hope you find that girl

Whose heart skips a beat

Every time you kiss her

The way that you kissed me

I hope you find that girl

Who dreams of you every night

Who thinks of you

Throughout her day

Just like I

I hope you find that girl

Who gives you

Your heart's desire

I only wish

I was that girl

To be your ever after.

Sunset

Come away with me

To a place only you and I know

A place where dreamers dream

And true lovers go

Let the sun kiss us on our skin

As we make love

Bathe in the rain

Under the stars above

Our moments together feel

So unreal

Drowned in your words

Finding solace under the moon

Your lips pressed against mine

Our passion could paint the sky.

Nectar

To feel you move within me

Awakens my soul

Exquisite sensation

Feels like I've found gold

The gentleness of your touch

The excitement of your voice

Trembling of our bodies

The sweetness of our skin

Kisses like honey

In a world with you only

You bring out the best

Like a magnet we connect.

Answer Me

You're my perfect dream

Would you shy away your feelings

Or come away with me

Don't leave me in this fairytale

Be my prince charming.

Here I Go Again

Is there a butterfly in my stomach

Cause I can't seem to think

Whenever you come around

My knees start to weak

The sensations of flutter

Start to pick up speed

Yes there is a butterfly

Possibly two or three.

Let's fall in love under the stars.

Against the Odds

Wish I could make you see

That you should be with me

I'll safeguard your heart

Love you eternally

Life is so short

But with you everlasting

Met by fate

But at the wrong time

Something inside tells me

Were destined to be

So take my hand

Don't let our love

Pass us by

We owe it to ourselves

To give it a try.

I don't like distance
I can't stand being apart
So be with me and only me
I'll safeguard your heart.

A life without butterflies...can't imagine.

Take this time
Let's unwind
Live in this moment
As if you were mine

Underneath these sheets
We're perfect.

I can't keep calm
I feel butterflies.

Love Quotes

Love

Never thought

That I could love someone

As much as I love you

You'll forever

Give me butterflies

With you my dreams come true.

Your First

Can't stand the thought

Of you with someone else

I wish that you were mine

If I had the power

I would turn back the hands of time

To meet you sooner

Imagine what that would be like

First kiss

First everything

Every moment I'll hold you tight.

Fire

I can feel your lips upon me

As I dream about you

Your scent still on my pillow

I love the smell of you

To be touched by you

Ignites me

You're the lighter

I'm the flame.

Another Time

Look up at the stars

Make a wish tonight

Wish that I was yours

I'll wish that you were mine

Time was the only thing

That kept us apart

Were perfect for each other

Wish we realized from the start

If I could hold you tight

I'd never let go

Kiss you a thousand times

As you make love to me slow

I want this

I want us

Can the world please stand still

So I can run to your arms

And tell you how I feel.

They feed off your love

Your love is what the butterflies crave.

You Are

You're the love of my life

You're the man of my dreams

You're my knight in shining armor

You're the song I'll always sing

My getaway… When nothing seems right

My protector… Through my darkest night

You hold the truth

You hold my heart in your hand

You're not only my lover

But my best friend

With you I don't worry

You wipe my tears every time

With you I have hope

Amongst the grayest skies

I'm yours till the end

I'm yours beyond this life

Forever devoted

Forever you and I.

Happy

I love the way

You make me feel

It's a feeling I can't explain

You excite every part of me

I hope you feel the same.

Daydreaming about you

Is my favorite thing to do

Got me singing love songs

I'm so into you.

Cheated

Guess I got to go

You got your plans

I got mine

Timing is everything

It was not on our side

Words put on hold

That may never be spoken

Tears filling my eyes

My heart is broken

Why can't this be our time

Is a question I'll always ask

How can you love someone

And not be with them

I hope this pain doesn't last.

Chemistry

Uncontrollable butterflies

I feel them all day

You have a hold on me

It's hard to explain

You excite my mind

You feed my soul

You're the one for me

Our love is like gold.

Questions

Will you love me

In the morning

Like you do at night

Will you love me

When the rain falls

Like you do

When the sun shines

Will you love me

Tomorrow

Like you love me today

Will you love me years from now

Will you love me day by day.

Your kisses are my favorite taste.

Time's Reason

If I could turn back The hands of time

I'd go back to when we first met

The feeling you gave me back then

Has never really left

I should have never let you go

Everything happens for a reason

Maybe one day will know

To have you close to me

Is what I'm longing for

The feel of your touch

The taste of your lips

The sound of your voice … Sweet reminisce

I remember like it was yesterday

The look in your eye

Too young to even try

Second chances are caused by fate

A reason unknown why

You're my person

I'm your person

I need you in my life

Dreamer's Heart

A dreamer's heart

Is always wishing

Wishing on that shooting star

Waiting for their long lost love

To rescue them from their prison of loneliness

A dreamer's heart

Is always hoping

Hoping for the day

When love will conquer all their fears

And chase their blues away

A dreamer will keep believing

No matter how hard it gets

With patience and virtue

Until a dreamer's heart is pure bliss.

What If

I saw your face among the crowd

It stopped me in my tracks

I stood there reminiscing

About the love that we once had

I started to smile … Then a tear fell down

Could not think of words to say

I wish things were different

I wish you could have stayed

What would we be like

Would we be happy in love

The look in your eye

Tells me you're still the one

The one that I still call on in my dreams

The one who slipped away

Without a proper goodbye

The one who gives me that feeling that hope is still alive

You approached me from that crowd

You wiped my tears away … Kissed my lips softly

I knew exactly what to say

I'll always love you

This feeling will never go away

Dreaming

When I dream of you

I pray it comes true

Because my dreams

Are the only place that I get to be with you

The joy I feel as I dream

Is a feeling I want to stay

But nights end

Mornings begin

Another day without you

Until I dream of you again.

I still get butterflies

When I think of you

See you

Touch you

Tell you I love you

over and over again.

The Standard

You held up a beauty

That was hard for me to see

You taught me how to trust

And believe in impossibilities

You gave me a reason

To keep pushing through

Helped me make it out of the storm

And for that

I thank you.

What happens if you don't feel butterflies ...

Do not worry ...

They're always there ...

they just have to be awakened.

With you I feel like
I can touch the sky
You give me a love
That takes me so high.

Lost in you
Awakened at the same time
Gentleness of your hands
Sweet taste of your lips
Time hold still
This is our moment

Keep touching my body
Your hands send sweet chills down my spine
My sensational desire
Your heart is what I'm after
Don't stop kissing me
You make the butterflies dance.

Love Quotes

Tonight in Love

Blame it on the moon in the sky

Blame it on the stars shining bright

Blame it on the slow song playing on the radio

That's got me in love with you tonight

Blame it on the butterflies I feel

First time I'm feeling something real

Blame it on the glisten I see looking in your eyes

That's got me in love with you tonight

Hoping that this night does not end

Funny how we started off as friends

Now you got me dancing to my favorite love song

That's got me in love with you tonight

Blame it on our hearts beating fast

Blame it on a love that could last

Blame it on your words spoken softly in my ear

That's got me in love with you tonight

Blame it on this night that we spent

Funny how it led to a kiss

Blame it on the passion I feel as you hold me tight

That's got me in love with you tonight

Blamed it on the moon in the sky

Waking up to the stars shining bright

Blame it on the feelings we've shared

Did not know was there

That's got us so in love tonight.

Only You

I want to be with you

Until the end of time

Spend every waking minute with you

Because you're all mine

No other person

Can make me feel the way you do

Your aura excites me

Your passion ignites me

I love the way you make me feel

Like a dream

But this is real.

Keep Me

I need you to stay

Or the butterflies will go

They'll never leave

As long as you love me so

Feel them flutter day and night

See them flutter in my dreams

Keep on loving me

Take me high

Like butterflies in the sky.

Be with that person
That gives you butterflies all the time.

A dreamer never sleeps
They wish all through the night
Wishing for their fairytale
Wishing with all their might

My hands start to shake
My knees start to weaken
The butterflies start to flutter
Loving you is the reason.

I can't get enough
Of the way you make me feel
The sensation of butterflies
What I feel is real
Together or apart
My love is here to stay
Nothing or no one can take that away.

Love Quotes

No Resistance

Show me that you're mine

Set my soul on fire

Touch every part of me

I'm yours to devour

Pour into me your love

I'll savor every kiss

Exhilarating passion

We simply can't resist.

Faith

You were there for me

At a time I needed you

You helped me see beauty within

And possibilities …I thought could never be achieved

You gave me a reason to

Believe

I can survive.

Yours

You can have me

Under the moonlight

You can have me

Under the stars

You can have me

In the gentle rain

As long as I'm in your arms.

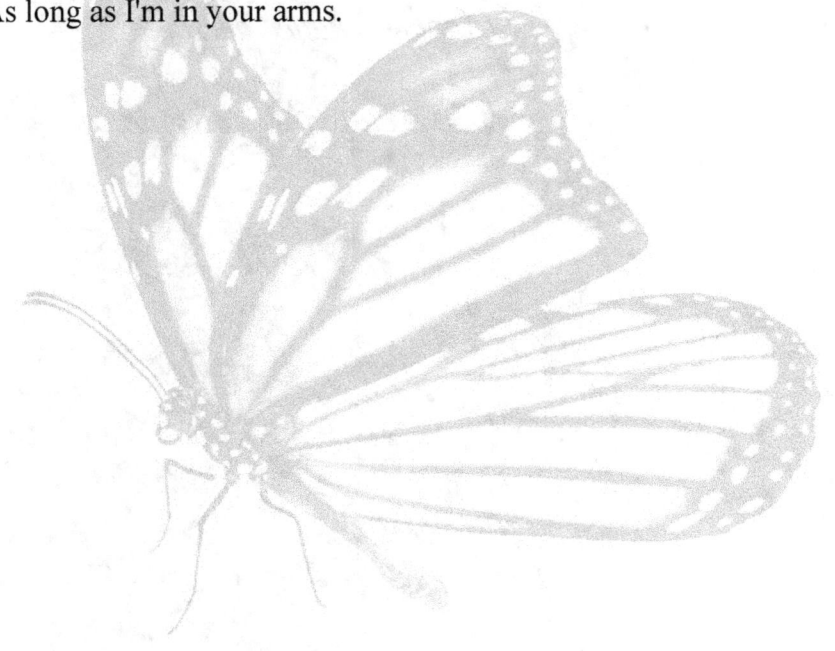

I took a chance on love

Because the butterflies told me so.

The best feeling in the world
Is the feeling I get
When I'm with you.

Touch my body
I want to feel
The gentleness of your hands
Look me in my eyes
You'll see my love has no end.

Love Quotes

No Distance

I trust your love

I know it's real

No matter how

Far we are apart

Days go by

Seasons change

But my love for you remains the same.

I hate saying goodbye

Not knowing when I'll see you next

Days

Weeks

Months

Feels like my heart

Has ripped out my chest.

In Love

I'm so lost without you

I don't know what to do

I wish I had you close to me

My heart is so in love with you

Your chivalry captures me

I'm smitten by your charm

Your voice is like poetry

I want to be forever in your arms

Distance keeps us apart

But our desire for each other

Keeps us so close.

Stay

Be with me

Under the moon and stars

Dance with me in the rain

Pull my body in close to yours

Take all my pain away.

Available

Play your favorite song

Pour us a glass of wine

I'm yours for the night

So please don't be shy

Have your way with me

Let our passion take control

Release all worries

My body is here to console

Like a damsel in distress

Let your love conquer my soul.

Committed

Someone that enjoys

Liking me

Loving me

Doing things with me

Letting their guard down

Being carefree

Someone who

Puts their all in every moment

Because we only experience it once.

In too deep
To turn and walk away
The butterflies I feel
Are making me stay.

If you ask me to stay
I promise I'll never leave.

Just the thought of you
Makes the butterflies come alive.

From the moment
You touched me
I was hooked on your love.

Love Quotes

Thick & Thin

You are mine

I am yours

In this big world

We found each other

You are everything to me and more

Some days are easy

Some days are hard

We always make it through

Our love is so strong

It's the greatest love story of all.

Never Ending

Dancing underneath the stars

The moon is the perfect light

I've always wished

For a moment like this

To be with you in the night and

Wake with you in the morning

Your love is like a river

It keeps flowing

So let the light of the moon

Kiss us on our skin

Make love to me under the stars

Over and over again.

My hero in disguise
The one who rescues me every time
My knight in shining armor
You loving me is an honor.

A love out of a story book
A love that's one of a kind
That's what you've given me
I'm so happy you are mine.

Love Quotes

Never Enough

I think about you

When I'm awake

I dream about you

When I sleep … 24/7 you're what I want

You're what I need

Thoughts of you

Fill my mind

Day dreaming of you all the time

I want you now

I want you here

Feel the butterflies

Inside of me

They flutter faster

When you're near

Your voice

Your touch

I just can't get enough

Everything about you excites me

No questions asked

You're the one.

I love your smell
I love your taste
Butterflies get excited
When they hear your name.

I want your lips
On every part of me
I want to feel you
Deep inside of me
You give me a rush
A passion
I can trust

I've been wishing
On a star
To find someone
And there you are.

Love Quotes

Wherever you go
My heart will follow.

Without You

My heart feels numb

My body feels empty

Can't sleep, can't think

I need you here with me

Nights are long

Days are slow

Time can only tell

Where our love will go.

Inspiration

It's you I want

It's you I need

Everything feels so right

When it's you and me

Feels like I can fly to the moon

Dance with the stars

That's how powerful

This love is of ours.

The Keys

You hold the key

To my heart

You have it on lockdown

No one could ever

Take your place

My love for you

Is here to stay.

Always

True lovers

Always find their way

In each other's arms

No matter the distance

No matter the length of time.

You held my hand, And said
You make me feel butterflies.

Union

Two souls connected

From the start

Distance means nothing

When the love

You have for them remains in your heart

Grateful

No matter what

I got you till the end

You're the best thing

That has happened to me

You're my lover

And my friend

You don't ever

Have to worry

My love will last a lifetime

Like the moon

In the sky

It will forever shine bright.

I Promise

I promise to love you

I promise to be true

I promise to be your safe place

When the world is no good to you

I promise to always hold you

And kiss you, everyday

I promise to be forever yours

And cherish our love each day.

Hold on to me tight
Never let go
This world can be so cold
But you keep me safe and warm.

Meeting you was
By accident
Falling in love
With you was unexpected.

Love Quotes

I Deserve

I deserve flowers

I deserve long walks on the beach

I deserve someone beyond good to me

I deserve passion

Like kissing in the rain

I deserve someone

Who loves me more and more each day

I deserve sweet words

Slow dances late at night

I deserve someone

Who holds me tight at night

I deserve a love

That's rare and hard to find

I deserve someone

Who is gentle and kind

Who is truthful and inspiring

Someone I can count on

No matter the timing

I deserve someone who looks at me and says

I'm yours forever darling

I'm yours till the end.

Think of Me

You awaken my soul

To feel something that

I've never felt before

A feeling so intense

Makes my heart reach

Out for more

I can feel it in your kiss

Goosebumps all over my skin

You're the one I want to be with

As if you were heaven sent

Being apart pains me

I told you before

I miss you like crazy

All I want to do

Is make love to you daily

So look up at the stars

And think of me before you sleep

We're perfect for each other

I want the world to see.

Meeting you was everything
A reason beyond my control.

Your Heart

I've never felt like this

Can't you see it in my eyes

And tell by my kiss

It's your heart

That I've been after

It's your heart I want to win.

Come Back

Silent cries to the moon

On a beautiful starry night

The air has a sweet warmth

That reminds me

Of you and I

As I lay in silence

I reminisce about our love

Every moment was breathtaking

Captured my heart and soul all at once

To not feel that feeling anymore

Saddens my heart

I'll keep crying tears to the moon

And wish on every star

That someday you will see

It is I that has your heart.

Telepathy

I wonder if you

Can see my thoughts

When I think of you

I wonder if you can hear

My heartbeat

When I kiss you

I wonder if you can feel the butterflies

I feel for you as you stare into my eyes

I wonder if you believe

My love is true

That you're the only person

I want to be with

The only person

I want

is you.

More butterflies please...

Inseparable

You and I

Against the world

Together forever

No one can come between us

You're all that I need

The air that I breathe

A love that I believe

Was destined to be.

Eternal

You're in my heart

You're here to stay

A love so strong

I can't let go

A love I always wanted

A love that grows and grows.

Completeness

With you I feel safe

With you I feel loved

With you impossibilities seem possible

The love we share is unstoppable

With you I can dream

Big dreams that I've never dreamt before

With you feels like home

No fear in growing old

With you my heart grows

More and more each day

With you is where I feel supported

Overjoyed and at peace

With you I found a reason

To always believe

That love always wins

It won with you and me.

Predestined

Met you unexpectedly

And unexpectedly I fell

Fell in love with you

I have no one to tell

Bottled up emotions

Sometimes I want to cry

Is it really wrong timing

Or not worth the try

I have my life

You have yours

But all I want

Is to hold you once more

Reasons we crossed paths

Who knows why

Laying up at night

Wishing you were mine

Connected souls

We were lovers from the start.

Orbit

Two lovers

Who dream the same dream

Whose hearts skip a beat

Every time that they meet

Their souls gravitate towards each other

Every time they touch and speak.

I want your heart
To be mine
I want my heart
To be yours.

I don't know
What the future holds
But I hope you're in it with me
Because the thought
Of not having you
Will destroy me completely.

Love Quotes

My Wish

Wishing on a falling star

Hoping that it reach your heart

All night

I pray

That you will stay

Here in my arms

Is where I want to be

I promise to love you forever

For all eternity.

Expression

Ever since the day

I saw you

I knew you were

The one for me

You gave me a reason to believe

Took my hand and showed me

This is how love should be.

Realization

It's been a while

Since you came around

I guess you finally see

That I was the girl for you

The one who appears in all your dreams

You left me without a say

And days and days went by

You'll never know the heartache and

All the tears I cried

I waited for you

And prayed at night

In hopes one day you see

That I was meant for you

And you were meant for me.

You give me a feeling
A feeling I can't shake
A feeling so amazing
I've never felt this way.

Tomorrow

The next time I see you

I'm running to your arms

When our two hearts connect

I feel as if

This is where I belong

The next time I see you

I'm holding you tighter

Kissing you longer

Making love to you stronger

The next time I see you

I know it won't be the last

For what we share together

Are some of the best moments

I've ever had.

Every kiss
Fills me up with butterflies.

My lips are drawn to yours
Your touch I always crave
Your presence arouses me
I love feeling this way.

In your arms
My heart perfectly fits
Stars shine bright
But our love shines brighter.

I can see it in your eyes
I can taste it upon your lips
You want this as much as I do
But you're afraid to admit.

Love Quotes

Happiness

You take my heartache away

You make me feel like a summer day

My rainbow after the storm

You clear up my cloudy days

The sound of your voice lights up my world

I'm so glad that I'm your girl

Forever and always

Just you and me

Peace and happiness

I believe we're meant to be.

A Moment

Hold on to this moment

I want this to last

You're the man of my dreams

Perfection

You and me.

Bliss

Making love all night

Till the morning

We got this special bond

That can't be broken

Sexual healing

Is what we do best

You give me a feeling

That I can't resist

All time high with you

I don't want to come down

Your love pours into me

I've fallen and drowned.

In a world of imperfections
You're perfect just for me.

Feel Me

My heart skips a beat
Every time that we meet
The kisses I give you
Take control of the words
I want to speak
I want to tell you my thoughts
And how they consume of you
That when I look up
At the stars at night
I wonder If you feel
The same as me too
Your hands upon my skin
Know how to pull me in
Your voice excites every part of me
These feelings I feel
Have no end
I want to be with you
In the sunrise
Make love to you
In the starry night
Your soul feeds my soul
My passion for you is so strong
In your arms is where I belong

Winning

My love

You have given me a love

That wishful lovers dream of

A love that will last a lifetime

No matter

The triumphs we may face

You're my person forever and always